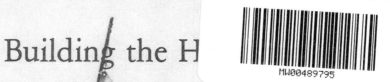

Building the H...

THE MANUFACTURERS METHOD

by BARRY THOMAS

Published by the Mystic Seaport Museum, Inc.

Mystic Seaport
75 Greenmanville Avenue
Mystic, CT 06355

Copyright © 1977 Mystic Seaport Museum,

Seventh Printing, 1999

ISBN 0-913372-33-1

CONTENTS

Herreshoff Small Boat Shop in the 1920s.
In the background dinghy molds are
set up with frames, floors, keel,
etc. in place, ready for planking.
A nearly completed boat is in the mid-
ground and a finished dinghy is in the
foreground. On the wall to the right
are other molds, patterns and battens.

INTRODUCTION

The age of fine yacht building began after the Civil War in the yards around City Island, New York; the Herreshoff yard at Bristol, Rhode Island; the Lawley yard on the South Shore of Boston. And it went Down East. The craft began its decline after World War I, and the decline was caused in part by the influences of the war. This was a decline in quality and the depression furthered it. Now with these yards gone - Lawley's, Herreshoff's, Nevins', and many smaller shops - the craft itself is virtually gone. Knowledge of it is now vestigial and third hand or worse.

It was therefore desirable for us at Mystic to attempt to make some record of boatbuilding at its prime - if a source could be found. Fortunately a source was found: a man who had built boats at Herreshoff's during that yard's prime. This provided us with a chance to make a unique entry in boatbuilding literature, for boatbuilding at Herreshoff's was unique.

Figure 1-1. Setup for Herreshoff 12 1/2-footers.

BACKGROUND I

T he Herreshoff method of building a boat consists of getting out a mold for each frame of the boat (every other frame in dinghies) and setting the molds upside down with the frames bent over the molds (See Figure 1-1). Building the hull upside down made much of the work easier and quicker -- planking, caulking, smoothing, and so on. This is a good production setup and if there is more than one boat to be built over a period of time, it can be reduced to a set of easily stored molds.

The boatbuilder who was our source is Charlie Sylvester. Charlie Sylvester began work at Herreshoff's in 1912 and left in 1940. To us it is amazing how much knowledge he retained of his craft, down to the smallest detail. Certainly he was very conscious of what he was about and honed his work so that it was logical and economical of time and movement. The results had to be good. Charlie Sylvester was not unique at that time, but was one of a number of men -- the "old fashioned mechanics" who, along with Mr. Nat, made the Herreshoff Manufacturing Company.

At yards such as Herreshoff's, one could find the very best inboard and outboard joiners, plankers, spar makers, pattern makers, foundry men, riggers, machinists, or whatever artisans were needed to build a boat. In breadth of experience and knowledge, such a yard was analogous to a university. There was much to learn and an interested man could gain a Ph.D's worth of knowledge and experience. These yards no longer exist in the United States, nor does the knowledge. This particular type of university is extinct.

The craft had its swan song in the late thirties. Only a few men are left who practice it -- the fits and the joinery, the fairness -- and most of the beauty of these boats is attributable to these men. The names of those who so impeccably fleshed out the idea, gave it substance, are forgotten. That is an injustice, but a common one. These men had a pride and love for their work, and a passionate and no doubt at times an imbalanced concern for its quality.

Charlie Sylvester figures that from 1920 to 1940, with the exception of the M.I.T. dinghies, he built nearly all the

Herreshoff dinghies. As a mechanic at Herreshoff's he also
had to put his hand to other jobs and thus was experienced
in operations in other areas of the yard.

SOURCES

All of the data in this report on building boats came
from Charlie Sylvester. Charles Sylvester was interviewed
by Maynard Bray and Barry Thomas. The interviews were
done in 1974 at Mr. Sylvester's house.

Charlie Sylvester began work at Herreshoff's in 1912, when
he was about 16 years old (see Figure 1-2). His father, who
died in 1905, had worked there before him and the family
had come to Bristol, Rhode Island, from South Bristol, Maine
The brother of Charles Sylvester's grandfather was the grandfather of Harvey Gamage, the South Bristol shipbuilder.

In 1924, owing to a business slump and the liquidation sale
of the company, Charles Sylvester and other Herreshoff Mfg.
Company employees found themselves without work. He subse-
quently returned to the Herreshoff Mfg. Company. During
the interim of less than a year, he had worked for Nevins
at City Island, N.Y. and for Nock in East Greenwich, R.I.
He left the Herreshoff Mfg. Company for good in 1940.

The other source for this subject was our own experience in
building a Herreshoff dinghy. This was a copy of an 11 1/2
foot *Columbia* lifeboat model dinghy (so named because the
first boat of this design was for the Cup Defender *Columbia*,
built in 1899) originally built in 1905. Although this is
several years before Charlie Sylvester's time at Herreshoff's
the 1905 dinghy supported what he told us in all respects.
Most photographs illustrating this paper record the building of the copy at Mystic Seaport in the winter of 1975-76.
The building of the replica enabled us to evaluate our
source and our understanding of our source.

HISTORICAL BACKGROUND

In *Traditions and Memories of American Yachting*, W. P.
Stephens describes the beginnings of a new method of setting up boats at Herreshoff's:

> In planning *Gleam*,* Nat adopted an original
> method of construction, a solid mould of two
> thicknesses of one-inch board was made for

* A catboat modeled in 1876.

2

Figure 1-2. Dinghy setup. The men are, left to right;
Ernest Alder, Charlie Sylvester, Henry Vincent, James
Clarkson, winter 1912-13. Alerion III in the background.

every frame, spaced about one foot apart. The two members of the frame were steamed and bent on the mould and held by dogs, their heels being united by a floor. With these moulds set up solidly on the keel, the planking was done more rapidly and more accurately than by the conventional method of frames bent to skeleton moulds and ribbands. *Sprite* presumably was set up with the keel on blocks and the moulds on the keel, but later this method was reversed, the moulds being made with the top edge as the baseline and set up directly on the floor upside down, the keel being laid on top of the moulds.

When he assumed an active part in the building Captain Nat built a separate mould for every frame, at spacings of 9 to 18 inches, according to the size of the yacht; the two members of the frame being bent on the mould and dogged fast; the moulds, at least treble in number over the old method, being set up on the keel and the planking begun. A few trials of this method led to a reversal of the process; the moulds were set up on the floor in inverted position and the keel laid on top of them; the planking following.

One advantage of this method was the ease of fitting the garboards, the workmen standing erect and working downward instead of crouching underneath and working upward. The laying of the broad strakes and the rest of the planking was similarly facilitated, the fastening was more easily done, and the "joining-off" and finishing the bottom, as well as the caulking where used, showed a greater gain in convenience and ease of working. On my first visit to Bristol in 1885 I was greatly impressed by the half dozen steam yachts then building by this method; the moulds, as I distinctly remember, were of two thickness of inch boards, crossing diagonally, each mould

of such depth that when set up on a level
floor the upper side conformed to the curve
of the keel. Why the moulds were made sol-
id I do not know, perhaps to give a better
base in bending, but this method was waste-
ful of lumber and was abandoned for the
conventional form of skeleton mould. Two
pieces of board were tacked together and
the outline scribed from the floor, the
pieces were cut out on a bandsaw, of course
identical in outline, and formed together
to make the mould. Experience proved that
a frame 2 by 2 inches could be bent around
the inch mould.

Thus it was W. P. Stephens who provoked the investigation
which resulted in this paper.

Nathanael Herreshoff designed boats by carving half
models which represented the boat to the outside of
the planking. Mr. Herreshoff used a special machine of
his own devising to take the offsets from the model.
These offsets were written down in a small brown book,
and this book was delivered to the mold loftsman who
"laid down" or drew the boat full size on the loft floor.
The boatbuilder "picked up" his patterns and molds from
this drawing. In the case of lapstrake dinghies, the
loftsman drew a section at every other frame, as there
is a building mold at every other frame. Thus in the
case of our 11 1/2-foot dinghy there were ten sections
on the lofted body plan.

The boatbuilder had a simple device for scribing the
shape of a mold from the body plan directly on the mold
itself. Since the frames were bent over the molds,
each mold must reflect the shape of the boat minus the
planking and the thickness of the frames (see Figure 2-1).

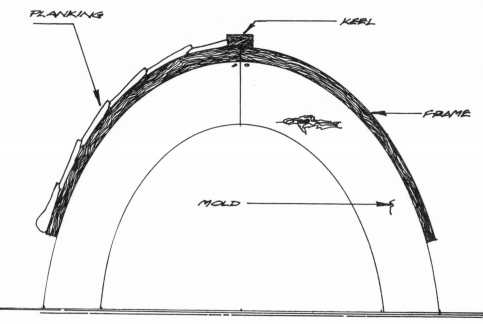

*Figure 2-1. The mold is the shape of the boat minus
frames and planking.*

The device used by the boatbuilder for scribing the
shape of the mold automatically deducted the planking
and the frame thickness. This tool is simplicity itself
(see Figure 2-2).

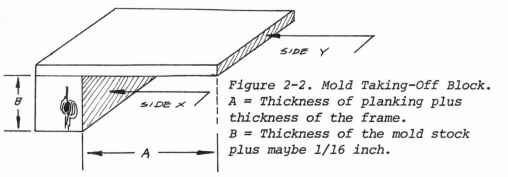

Figure 2-2. Mold Taking-Off Block.
A = Thickness of planking plus
thickness of the frame.
B = Thickness of the mold stock
plus maybe 1/16 inch.

Charlie Sylvester had a definite, careful procedure for
taking off the shape of a mold and for making both sides
of the mold exactly alike. Because it is a well-thought
out procedure, it is worth noting. First, the pieces to
make one-half of the mold were put on the lofted body
plan. When put together, the outside edge of these
pieces must be no farther from the section on the body
plan than the thickness of the planking and the molded
thickness of the frame (see Figure 2-3).

The mold pieces must have a good joint between them.
They are then pulled together with dogs, temporarily
nailed to the body plan floor (i.e. the board or floor
on which it is drawn), and temporarily fastened together
with a cleat or butt block. Now the frame section is
marked on the assembled half mold using the mold taking-
off block. Side "X" of the block (see Figure 2-2) is
placed along the section line of the body plan (see Figure 2-3). Then mark the mold pieces using side "Y" of
the block as a guide. A series of marks is made from
the keel of the section to the base line. These marks
are then joined by pencil after having sprung in a suit-
ably stiff batten as a guide. Then the following lines
are squared up from the body plan and carefully struck
across the mold: base line (or floor line), sheer line,
and, if desired, the load waterline. Also a witness
mark (sirmark) is struck in where the two half molds
join at the keel.

The half mold is now carefully picked up from the floor
and to its underside are screwed enough pieces, well

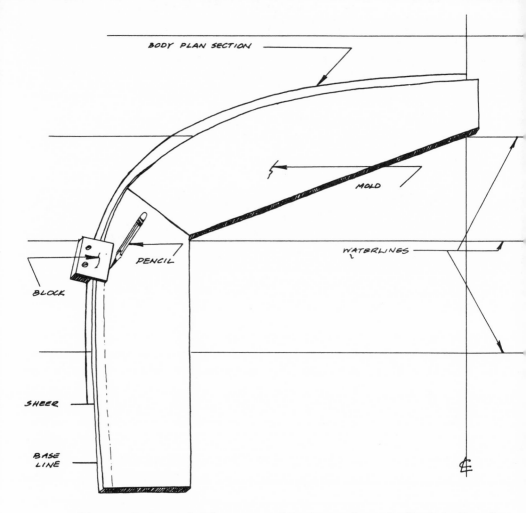

BODY PLAN SECTION

MOLD

WATERLINES

PENCIL

BLOCK

SHEER

BASE
LINE

℄

Figure 2-3. Picking up mold shape from lofted body plan.

joined, to make the other half of the mold. The outside edge of the mold is then cut on the bandsaw, both
sides being thus cut at once. This edge is then joined
off fairly with a smoothing plane, square and to the
line.

The base line, sheer line, load waterline, and witness
mark are now squared across the other half of the mold.
Temporary cleats are placed on the other half mold. The
two halves are then separated from each other.

On the sides opposite the temporary cleats, the final
cleats are fastened; this is done on both halves (so that
after beveling the edge of the mold, the original pencil
line put on when picking up the mold will be retained).

The molds are put together side by side. At the keel end
of the mold, the witness marks are lined up. At the upper ends of the mold halves, a "sheer band" (cross spall)
with the breadth of the mold and centerline marked on it
is fastened, thereby correctly spacing the mold breadth.
A cleat is also fastened to the halves at the keel end
of the mold. The whole mold is now assembled.

The top of the keel must be accurately marked and cut for
on the mold. This is done as follows: A batten is made
up on which are marked the distances from the base line
to the top of the keel at each frame station. The distances are ticked off from the lofting.

A sort of "T" square is temporarily nailed snug up
against the ends of the mold (see Figure 2-4). The angle
in the "T" carries the base line athwart the mold, and
the batten with the base line to keel distances can thus
butt against the base line, and the distance can be
struck off on the mold. The mold is then cut off square
along the keel line.

Steel angle irons are then bolted to the molds at
the base line. These angles are used to screw the
molds to the shop floor.

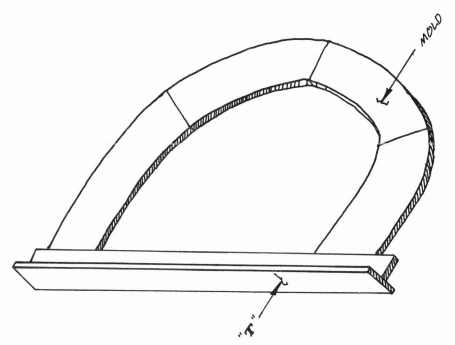

Figure 2-4. T-square for measuring off keel depths.

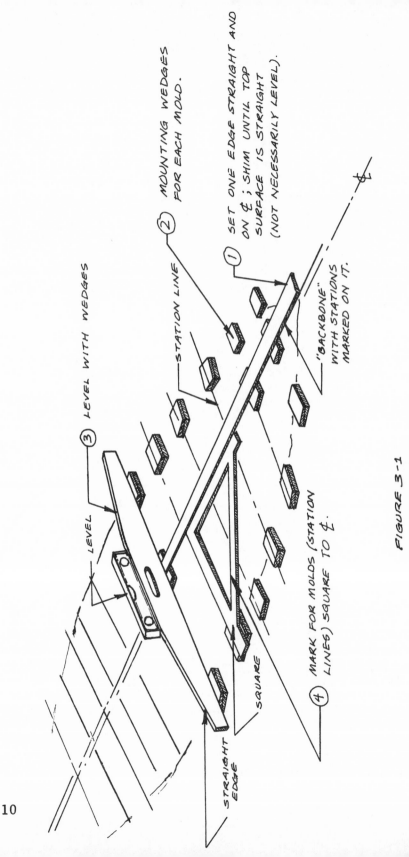

② MOUNTING WEDGES FOR EACH MOLD.

① SET ONE EDGE STRAIGHT AND ON ℄; SHIM UNTIL TOP SURFACE IS STRAIGHT (NOT NECESSARILY LEVEL).

℄

"BACKBONE" WITH STATIONS MARKED ON IT.

STATION LINE

③ LEVEL WITH WEDGES

LEVEL

SQUARE

④ MARK FOR MOLDS (STATION LINES) SQUARE TO ℄.

STRAIGHT EDGE

FIGURE 3-1

THE FOUNDATION

TO ACHIEVE A PLANE SURFACE ON WHICH TO SET UP THE BOAT

10

LAYING THE FOUNDATION   III

The "foundation" is shown in Figure 3-1. The boat is built on the foundation which, regardless of the unevenness of the floor, provides a flat plane on which to build the boat. First the "backbone" (1, Figure 3-1) batten is nailed to the shop floor. One edge of the backbone is to be the centerline of the boat, so that edge must be made straight. As the floor probably has dips and humps in it, the backbone must be shimmed up here and there so that it is straight on top, for its top surface is the base line of the boat. The backbone is securely nailed down and the nails set. A straight edge, chalked on its bottom, is then placed on the backbone and moved back and forth a bit. The high spots thus chalked are planed off and this process repeated until the backbone is straight on top.

The ten mold stations are then marked on the backbone. Using a square, these stations are then squared out on either side of the centerline. The distance from the centerline to the angle brackets on each mold are ticked off on a stick. These distances are then marked out from the centerline on the station lines just squared out. A pair of wedges is placed at these distances; the brackets on the molds will rest on these wedges.

The foundation must be level athwartships (there is no need to be level fore and aft). To this end a level is placed across the backbone at each station, and the wedges on either side are adjusted to obtain a level line from wedge to backbone to wedge (see Figure 3-1). When the wedges are properly adjusted they are driven together about another quarter of an inch and nailed down to the floor with the nails set in. Using the level as a guide, the tops of the wedges are planed down until there is again a level line across the top of the wedges and backbone. Wedges are thus placed and leveled for all station molds.

This is the complete foundation and it is now ready to receive the molds.

SETTING UP AND BEVELING THE MOLDS

The next step is to set up the molds starting with the widest or midship mold. With the mold in its appropriate place on the foundation, a straight edge is lined up vertically on the centerline of the mold (see Figure 4-1).

With the straight edge extending down to the backbone, the mold is moved athwartships until the straight edge lines up the mold centerline, with the centerline represented by the backbone. With this done and the mold square to the centerline, the angle irons on either side of the mold are screw-fastened down through the wedges into the floor.

Where the shape of the boat is getting smaller going forward, the molds are placed forward of the station line and where the boat diminishes going aft, the molds are put on the aft side of the station line. This is to allow beveling wood for beveling the molds. In addition, the "smooth side" of the molds is always on the station line. This means that the line originally scribed on the mold will not be beveled off and lost.

For the 11 1/2-foot dinghy, mold 6 was chosen as the midship mold and screwed down first. Then molds 5 and 4 were set up. Two shores were nailed to the midship mold (one to port and one to starboard). These shores go through molds 5 and 4 and land on the floor of the shop. Using a large square, the midship mold is squared to the backbone and the shores are then nailed to the floor, thereby holding the mold in place (see Figure 4-2).

Two molds are then set up on the other side of the midship mold and then the midship mold is shored from that side. All the remaining molds are then set up. These are squared to the backbone by measuring the frame spacing starting from the shored up midship mold and working fore and aft. The spacing is maintained by a batten nailed to the midship mold and then to each succeeding mold as it is properly spaced. This is not the final adjustment of the frame spacing -- that comes after the keel is bent over the molds.

Since the boat narrows fore and aft from the midship

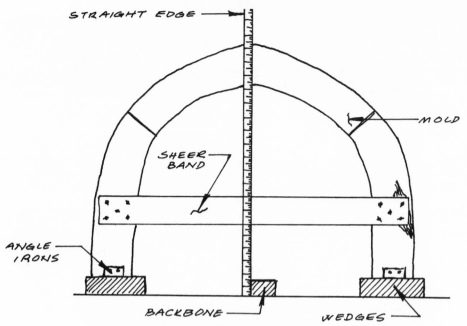

Figure 4-1. Lining up mold athwartships.

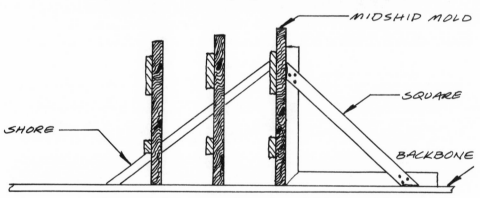

Figure 4-2. Squaring the midship mold.

mold, the molds must be beveled so that the frames, when
they are bent on the molds, will lie square to the planking. (In some cases, Herreshoff yachts have frames that
are beveled on their outboard face and parallel to the
fore and aft centerline on their inboard side. These
frames were obviously bent on square-edged molds, a
method Charlie Sylvester was not familiar with.) Using
a stiff batten as a guide, the molds are beveled with a
spokeshave and plane so that the batten lies full and
fair on the molds.

Now the boat itself can be built. The molds are removed
from the foundation so the frames can be steamed over them.

13

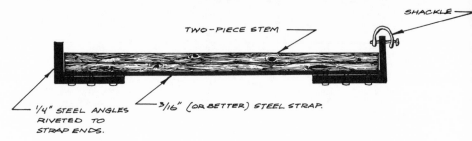

Figure 5-1. Steel strap for steam bending stem.

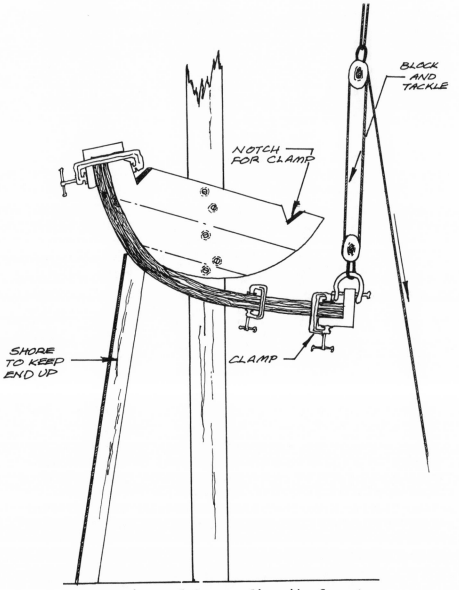

Figure 5-2. Bending jig for stem.

GETTING OUT THE FRAME V

At Herreshoff's, the "frame" of a boat was her stem, keel, transom, frames, and floors.

THE STEM

When Charlie Sylvester was building dinghies, the stem piece was steam bent to shape out of one piece. The dinghy which we copied had a stem bent out of two pieces. This, plus the fact we bent a single piece which broke and bent a double-piece stem which was good, decided us to use the two-piece stem. The stem is clamped in a steel strap (see Figure 5-1).

The stock for the stem is unseasoned, straight-grained white oak. The two-piece stem (or stem plus apron) is sided 1 3/4 inches and molded 2 1/4 inches. The stock which is steam bent is 3/4 inch more in the molded direction and about 1/2 inch more in the sided direction than the finished stem.

The oak is given more of a bend than is required for the finished stem. This allows for the slight springing back of the oak when it is removed from its bending form. Just how much overbend is put into a piece of oak depends in some degree on the stock and requires an experienced guess. Thus, with the piece overbent and oversized, the pattern can be put on the rough steam-bent piece to advantage, adjusted as necessary and the piece cut to final shape.

At Herreshoff's yard the jig for bending the stem was as shown in Figure 5-2. At Mystic, we did the same thing except that the jig was spiked to the floor.

The oak was steamed for about two hours and then taken from the steam box and placed in the steel strap. When bending something of this size over a tight curve, it is essential to compress the ends of the piece. This can be done by having the piece fit snugly between the ends of the strap. If the piece is not long enough, a block of oak can be fitted to fill the gap. We C-clamped the oak to the strap and then slowly began to bend it around the form, removing claps as they got in the way. The end is finally clamped to the jig.

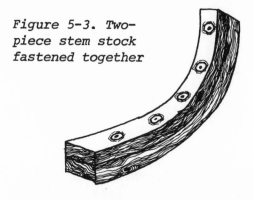

Figure 5-3. Two-piece stem stock fastened together

A few days later the stem pieces are removed from the bending form and screwed together from the inside: this locks the stem into its curve (see Figure 5-3).

There may be some twist in the stem piece so it is joined or planed flat and straight on one side. Then the other side is planed in the thickness planer until the stem is down to its correct sided dimension. Now the stem pattern is placed on the stem piece to advantage, and the molded shape of the stem is marked down. The stem is then cut to shape on the bandsaw. The rabbet is marked on the stem.

At Mystic the stem rabbet was cut out on the bench. At Herreshoff's, however, the stem rabbet was first roughed out on a shaper and then finished when in place on the boat. Charlie Sylvester used a batten, the end of which was the thickness of the plank, and a rounded chisel (see Figure 5-4) and rabbet plane to work the rabbet.

Figure 5-4. Charlie Sylvester's chisel for cleaning out rabbets.

The batten was sprung over the molds and offered to the outside rabbet line on the stem, and the notch made by the shaper was cleaned out until the batten end fit -- not much of a job for 1/4 inch planking. They always held to the <u>outside</u> rabbet line which was marked on the stem and keel.

THE KEEL

The keel for the boat built at Mystic was a flat plank keel for a centerboard sailing dinghy. The keel for a dinghy without a centerboard seems generally to be a

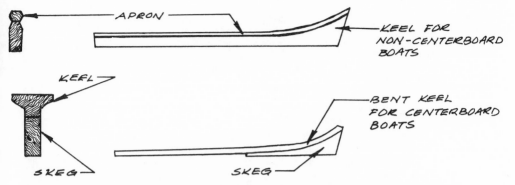

Figure 5-5. Keel construction for centerboard and non-centerboard boats.

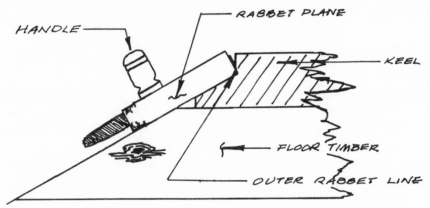

Figure 5-6. Rabbet plane for cutting keel rabbet.

plank on edge which incorporates the skeg and takes an "apron" piece on top (see Figure 5-5).

The keel is of oak, one inch thick and cut to shape in the half-breadth view. The rabbet is rough cut on the shaper.

Later, when the keel is sprung over the molds and fastened to the floor timbers, a rabbet plane is used to finish the rabbet. One side of the plane is laid flat on the frames and floor timbers, and the rabbet is cut in square to the frames until the outer rabbet line is reached (see Figure 5-6).

After the rough rabbet is cut in the keel, a form is made for the upwards curve of the keel aft. This form exaggerates the curve for over-bending. The after end of the keel is then steamed and clamped to the form where it stays until it is time to put it over the molds.

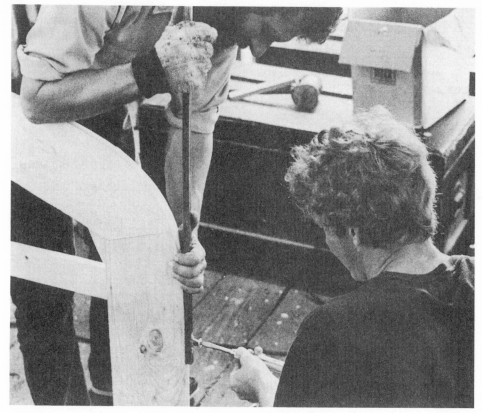

Figure 5-7. Fastening hot frame to mold.

TRANSOM

The transom was got out of mahogany. The original boat had an oak transom and sheer strake, and butternut thwarts. However, as the Herreshoff yard either finished the boat in oak and butternut or mahogany trim, or sometimes teak, we chose mahogany as we lacked seasoned oak. The transom bevels were done with the transom in place, using a batten across the molds and transom as a guide.

FRAMES

The molds are of 7/8-inch pine. On the outside beveled edge of each mold, a line 1/2 inch (the thickness of a frame) is scribed out from the smooth side of the mold. A few nails were driven in the mold along this line to prevent the frames from slipping down the bevel and off the station line.

The frames were 1/2-inch square white oak. They are

Figure 5-8. Frames dogged down on molds.

steamed about 30 minutes and then bent over the molds.
The molds are placed near the steam box. A cleat is
nailed to the floor so that the angle irons on the mold
can be shoved under it to help hold the mold while bending the frame (see Figure 5-7).

Charlie Sylvester also had a word to say about steam.
The steam is to be wet steam and lots of it. This means
that pressure in the steam box is undesirable. Nor was
anything added to the boiling water (e.g. soap or kero-
sene).

The hot frame is pulled from the box and one end fastened above the sheer line on the mold. A screw is used
for this or sometimes the mold has a metal strap around
the edge, through which the frame is thrust and then
wedged in. The frame is then bent along the mold and
dogged down where needed; at the most, two dogs per frame
are needed (see Figure 5-8). The framing dogs used at

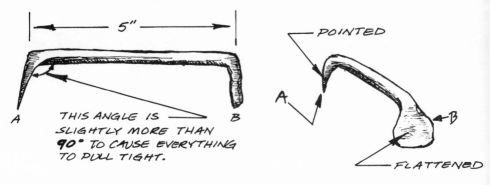

Figure 5-9.   Framing dog.

Herreshoff's were made out of mild steel rod and looked as shown in Figure 5-9.

Bending the frames over the molds took less than an hour. The next step was to fasten the floor timbers to the molds.

FLOOR TIMBERS

The floor timbers were 5/8-inch thick and 1 1/8-inches deep of seasoned white oak. Stock for the floor timbers was placed against the appropriate mold and the outline of the frames and bottom of the mold was scribed on the floor. This, of course, is the shape of the floor; how-ever, the floor lies on that side of the mold where the bevel increases (see Figure 5-10).

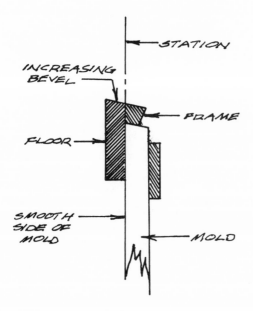

Figure 5-10.
Smooth side of the mold.

20

The floor must not be cut out to the line, but cut with enough wood left for the bevel. The floor is then riveted to the frames, two rivets per frame. The bevel is then cut on the floor timbers, using the frames as a guide. The bevel for the bottom of the floor is obtained from the profile of the keel on the lofting.

SETTING UP

The molds with their frames and floors in place are set up on their respective wedges and screwed down again. The midship mold must be squared to the backbone and shored up as before.

A batten is used to pick up the station spacing at the top of the keel from the lofting. The outside of the transom, and the forward end of the keel are also marked on the batten, and the centerboard case slot as well. These marks are transferred to the keel and squared across it. The centerboard case slot is cut out.

After the transom knee and transom are screwed together, the knee is fastened to the keel, the stem is fastened to the keel, and the keel is sprung over the molds. The keel is adjusted fore and aft until its midship station line is lined up with the smooth side of the midship mold; that is, between the floor and frame (see Figure 5-11).

The keel is then clamped to the midship floor or temporarily toenailed in place. Each floor is permanently fastened to the keel with one screw on either side of the boat's centerline, going from the keel into the floor.

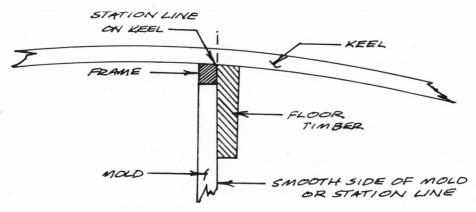

Figure 5-11. Station line.

The rest of the molds (those not being shored up) are lined up with their respective marks on the keel and fastened.

The top of the transom is then lined up plumb over the centerline represented by the backbone on the floor and made square to the backbone as well. It is then fastened to the shop floor (see Figures 5-12 and 5-13).

Using a batten across the aftermost frames and the transom, the bevel is cut on the transom. The tools are a spokeshave and a small "baby" plane (Stanley 101). The rabbet of the keel is cut using a rabbet plane as before-mentioned, and the stem rabbet is finished with a curved chisel and a rabbet plane.

Figure 5-12. Boat ready for planking (forward).

Figure 5-13. Boat ready for planking (aft).

PLANKING VI

With the boat set up, the "frame" of the boat ready, and the rabbet cut, she is ready to be planked. Planking for the boat built at Mystic was 1/4-inch Eastern white cedar. The general rule for lap width is twice the thickness of the planking, which meant a 1/2-inch lap in the boat at Mystic. This means that the spiling must be very accurate, as with such a narrow lap, the plank cannot be adjusted up and down on the lap very much, nor can the plank be edge-set much, as this prevents the laps from coming together.

KNOTS AND PLUGGING KNOT HOLES

All black knots must be removed and plugged. The knot holes are reamed out but never so much as to take out the hard wood surrounding the knot. The plug is whittled out, dipped in orange shellac, and twisted snug in the hole with the grain 90 degrees to the plank grain. The small end is then cut off leaving 3/8 inch standing. This is finely split and a thin wedge inserted to spread the end. The wedge should enter about half-way into the plug. The plug is then cut flush and sanded, this operation being done on the bench.

LINING OFF THE PLANK

The basic decision to make is how many planks will be used to close up a side of the boat. First, the underside edge of the sheer strake must be decided upon and the top of the garboard as well.

Most of these dinghies had 10 planks to a side; a larger dinghy, say an 18-footer, of course, had more. The sheer strake, because of its molded shape, is made wider than the strakes below it. It should be wider by about 1/2 inch. With this in mind, a batten is tacked to the frames to represent the underside of the sheer strake. When this is satisfactory, the underside of the sheer plank is marked on the frames. The top of the garboard is also decided with a batten, the garboard being given as much width as seems judicious, maybe 4 3/4 inches amidships in a 12-foot boat.

The widths of the remaining planks now must be decided.
As the boat is straighter on its bottom or deadrise,
the planks should be wider there, and on the curve
of the bilge they should be narrower; the tighter or
harder the bilge, the narrower the planks. Charlie
Sylvester decided the rest of the plank widths by
using a planking scale. This planking scale was
shown to him by a boatbuilder at Nevins'. Charlie
never showed it to anyone until he was interviewed
by the museum. Many techniques were commonly trade
secrets and seldom divulged.*

The plank widths were apportioned as follows: At
each mold, Charlie Sylvester would tick on a batten
the distances between the top of the garboard and
the bottom of the sheer plank. Then, having determined how wide the planks were to be on the midship
mold, he would draw up the planking scale shown in
Figure 6-1. Then he would write the plank widths
on a sheet of paper and destroy the scale.

At Mystic we added a step which Charlie Sylvester,
in his experience, did not use. We drew the midship
section on a board and on this drew the planks and
their laps. The broad strakes were made wide so as
to get narrower planks on the turn of the bilge.
These midship widths were then laid off on line AB
in Figure 6-1.

SPILING

As the planks of a boat are all curved and tapered, and
each plank (on one side) has a curve different from any
other plank on that side (see Figure 6-2), the shape of
the edge of each plank must be accurately determined.
The method for doing this is called spiling.

The garboard is spiled in the conventional way using a
compass. The spiling for the remaining planks is different and very fast.

The spiling batten is placed on the boat and nailed down
(using small nails), or clamped so that the batten lays

*This is not owing to an attribute of quaintness. What
a craftsman knew was his power and security, as is money
to a wealthy man; a craftsman might be as chary of his
knowledge as another man might be with his money.

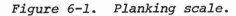

Figure 6-1. Planking scale.

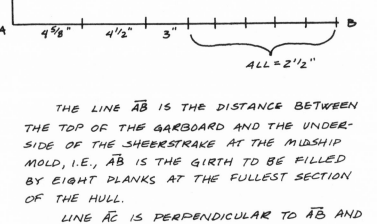

THE LINE $\overline{AB}$ IS THE DISTANCE BETWEEN THE TOP OF THE GARBOARD AND THE UNDER-SIDE OF THE SHEERSTRAKE AT THE MIDSHIP MOLD, I.E., $\overline{AB}$ IS THE GIRTH TO BE FILLED BY EIGHT PLANKS AT THE FULLEST SECTION OF THE HULL.

LINE $\overline{AC}$ IS PERPENDICULAR TO $\overline{AB}$ AND OF ARBITRARY LENGH, SAY THREE FEET. THE LONGER $\overline{AC}$ IS, THE MORE ACCURATE THE SCALE IS.

LINE $\overline{AB}$ IS DIVIDED INTO EIGHT PLANK WIDTHS. THE WIDTH OF $4^{5}/8''$ (THE ACTUAL PLANKING SCALE IS NOT DRAWN TO SCALE BUT IS FULL-SIZE) IS THE WIDTH OF THE BROAD STRAKE, THE FIRST PLANK NEXT TO THE GARBOARD. THE $4^{1}/2''$ WIDTH IS THE SECOND BROAD STRAKE; THE 3" WIDTH, THE THIRD, AND THE $2^{1}/2''$ WIDTHS ARE THE FIVE TOPSIDE PLANKS.

26

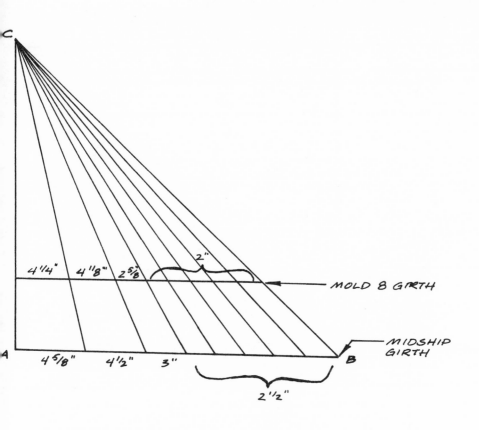

EACH OF THE PLANK WIDTH MARKS ON THE
MIDSHIP MOLD GIRTH ($\overline{AB}$) IS CONNECTED TO
POINT C ON $\overline{AC}$. NOW THE BATTEN UPON WHICH
THE GIRTHS OF THE MOLDS ARE MARKED IS
PLACED ON THE SCALE AND, KEEPING THE
BATTEN PARALLEL TO $\overline{AB}$, IT IS MOVED UP UNTIL
THE GIRTH OF THE MOLD IS REACHED, AND
IS LIMITED BY LINES $\overline{AC}$ AND $\overline{BC}$ AS SHOWN
ABOVE. A LINE IS STRUCK REPRESENTING THE
GIRTH OF MOLD B. THE PLANKING WIDTHS
FOR THIS MOLD CAN THEN BE MEASURED
DIRECTLY FROM THIS LINE. THE PLANKING
WIDTHS AT ALL MOLDS ARE HANDLED IN
THIS FASHION.

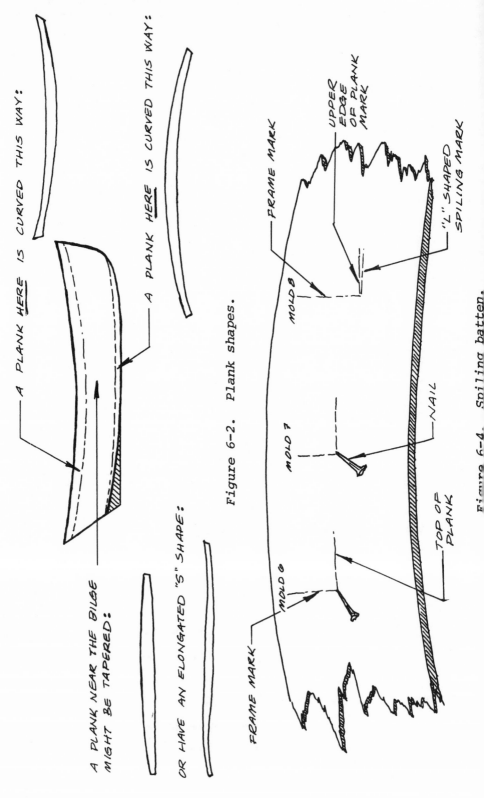

A PLANK HERE IS CURVED THIS WAY:

A PLANK HERE IS CURVED THIS WAY:

A PLANK HERE

A PLANK NEAR THE BILGE MIGHT BE TAPERED:

OR HAVE AN ELONGATED "S" SHAPE:

Figure 6-2. Plank shapes.

FRAME MARK

MOLD 8

UPPER EDGE OF PLANK MARK

"L" SHAPED SPILING MARK

MOLD 7

NAIL

MOLD 6

FRAME MARK

TOP OF PLANK

Figure 6-4. Spiling batten.

28

fair on the lap of the last plank put on the boat (see Figure 6-3). There must be no edge set in the batten.

At each frame from inside the boat, a pencil line is run along the top edge of the last plank put on the boat and up along the frame, thus forming an L-like mark. The forward end of the plank is also marked on the batten. The spiling batten is then placed on the plank board (see Figure 6-4), and through the point of each "L" a small finishing nail is driven right through to the plank board beneath. The batten is then removed and the holes in the plank board are joined by a fairly sprung batten to get the bottom shape of the next plank to go on the boat.

The widths of the plank are obtained from the planking scale or diminishing batten, and these are laid off on the plank at each mold station. A batten is then fairly sprung through these marks to form the upper edge of the plank.

Figure 6-3. Spiling batten on boat.

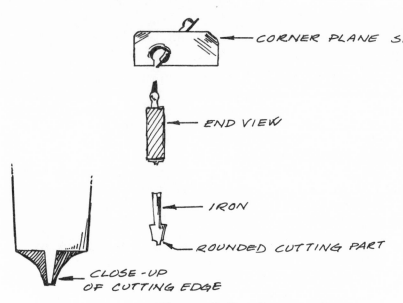

Figure 6-5. Corner plane.

Now with the plank having been spiled onto a 7/8-inch board, the plank shape is cut out on a bandsaw. (We find at Mystic that planks are more easily cut out on a table saw with its blade adjusted so that it just clears the top of the board being cut.) The edges are now joined square with a smoothing plane right to the line. As the inside upper plank edge is rounded off on each plank, the rounding off is done at this point. The tool Charlie Sylvester used for this was a "corner plane" (see Figure 6-5). Because of the double-bitted iron, this plane could be used fore or aft on either side of the boat.

The top outside edge of this board (this will be the upper inside edge of the plank in the boat) is then rounded with the corner plane but short of where the gain* or rabbet is to be cut in either end of the plank. The plank is then resawed on the bandsaw and planed smooth to thickness.

BEVELING THE LAPS

Having got out the plank to shape, the next step is to bevel the lap. The top edge of every plank has an unchanging bevel planed on it. In this case, the bevel

---

* The gain is a notch cut in the ends of the plank to allow the overlapping planks to fit flush at the stem and transom.

Figure 6-6. Lap plane.

is 1/2 inch wide and 1/16 inch deep. This bevel is cut using a special lap plane that automatically planes the bevel to the correct width and depth. This plane is shown in Figure 6-6.

We at Mystic made our own lap plane, copied exactly from Charlie Sylvester's, except that ours was for a narrower lap. In the case of the garboard, this bevel is planed only on the top. The bottom of the garboard is square and comes against the keel rabbet and is screwed into the back rabbet. The next plank will have the bevel planed on both edges.

Now, because the side of the boat curves and because this curve changes, the bevel of the two planks much change. The bevel is adjusted in the following way: Assume there there is a plank on the boat. A fid stick is then made ("fid" is probably a corruption of "fit"). This is a piece of wood as thick as the plank (1/4 inch) and about as long as the next plank to go on the boat is wide. The width of the fid stick is arbitrary, say about 1/2 inch to 5/8 inch. On one end of this stick, plane the same bevel that the lap plane automatically cuts on the laps. Now, this fid stick is placed on each frame with its bevel coming down on the lap of the plank on the boat. The fid stick represents the next plank to go on the boat (see Figure 6-7).

Using the fid stick as a gauge, the lap bevel of the

Figure 6-7. Gauging the plank lap with the fid stick.

Figure 6-8. Planing the lap bevel to fit.

plank on the boat is planed down until the fid stick
lap lays perfectly on the plank lap. This is done at
each frame, taking care to keep the changing bevel from
frame to frame fair (see Figure 6-8).

Notice that the plane used was a Stanley 101, or baby
plane. When the lap was finally adjusted, Charlie Sylvester took a final shaving off the bevel with a convex, low-angle block plane. This plane is made slightly
convex with a file and smoothed with sandpaper. This
means that the laps are slightly hollow and will be
pulled tight by rivets. Laps that are convex are no
good (see Figure 6-9).

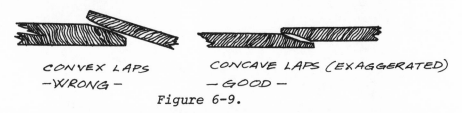

CONVEX LAPS
—WRONG—

CONCAVE LAPS (EXAGGERATED)
—GOOD—

Figure 6-9.

Now, the next plank with its unchanging bevel, as cut
by the lap plane, can be hung on the boat and the laps
should fit perfectly. Of course, the planks are finish-
sanded on both sides before they are hung on the boat.

CUTTING THE GAIN

At the stem rabbet and at the transom the lapped planks
must be gradually let into each other so that they lie
flush on the inside (see Figure 6-10).

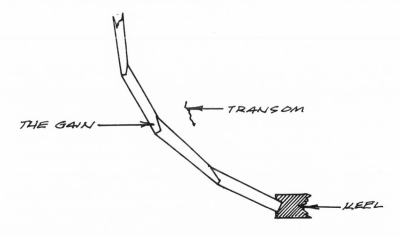

THE GAIN

TRANSOM

KEEL

Figure 6-10. Plank ends at the transom: the gains.

Figure 6-11. Cutting a gain.

The way Charlie Sylvester cut a gain was quick and simple. The length of the gain is about 6 inches. The thicker the plank the longer the gain. A straight edge is placed along the lap where the gain is to be cut. This straight edge is to guide the rabbet plane as it cuts the lap (see Figure 6-11).

The gain is roughed out with a chisel and finished with a rabbet plane. The gain on the upper inside of the plank must come to a feather edge.

Figure 6-12 shows the completed gain. Note a thin board is placed under the gain to support the feather edge while cutting it.

HANGING THE PLANK

The plank is now ready to be hung. It is placed in position on the boat. The forward end is quickly trimmed so that it fits in the stem rabbet and the plank clamped in place. The plank is fastened with screws to the stem rab-

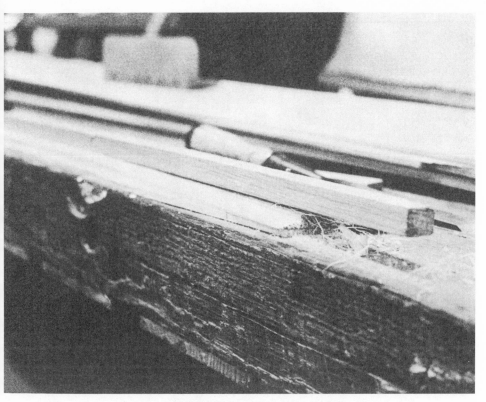

Figure 6-12. The gain.

bet. Holes are drilled through the laps about every two inches for the lap nails, leaving a space for the intermediate frames which are to be put in after the boat is planked. These are Number 14 copper nails, and the holes must not be too large or too small but allow for the nails to be tapped firmly through the laps. All of the lap nails are now put through the laps but are not yet riveted. All the riveting is done when the boat is turned right side up.

On each frame, the upper lap of the plank is fastened down with a 3/8 inch brass escutcheon pin. This fastening will remain in the boat but will later be reinforced with a rivet after the boat is turned right side up. Until that time, only the escutcheon pins will be holding the frames to the planks.*

* At Mystic, as can be seen in the photographs, the copper nails through the laps and frames were drilled

Figure 6-13. Stern caulking and gain.

Between the plank and the transom a strand of cotton is laid, outboard of the screw fastenings into the transom (see Figure 6-13).

Each plank is done in this fashion. The sheer-strake molding is done with a concave plane, a convex plane, a scraper cut to conform to the molding, and finally sanded with a block that was cut to the shape of the

- - - -

for and inserted as each plank went on. This was not done because we thought it better, but through a misunderstanding. Of course, nails must not go into the molds. The best way is to put the frame nails in after the boat is right side up with the molds removed. Then the nail hole can be drilled from the inside through the frame first; drilling otherwise, it is very difficult to get the hole to come out the other side in the dead center of the frame.

molding. At Herreshoff's, of course, they had a shaper to cut the molding.

At Mystic we had some difficulty with the sheer strake which Charlie Sylvester does not remember having had. The problem was this: A spiling was made for the sheer strake and a 1/4-inch thick plank was cut to this shape and temporarily hung on the boat. We did this to ensure that the sheer strake would look right. This 1/4-inch plank was used as a pattern to put the shape on the mahogany plank. The mahogany plank was cut out and the typical Herreshoff molding worked on it and hung on the boat, and at either end of the boat the plank lacked enough curve to come up to the sheer by an inch or more. The reason for this, we deduced, is that the neutral axis of a plank with a cross section like this

will cause a bend different from a plank with a cross section like this.

We used the first attempted sheer strake as a spiling batten for another try and the sheer strake then fitted perfectly.

COMPLETING THE BOAT

After the dinghy is planked, it is turned right side up and set on two horses which are nailed to the floor. Light nails are then toenailed up through the horses into the keel, thus securing the boat to the horses.

The boat is then leveled athwartships, shored up, and any twist taken out of it in the following manner: using a carpenter's level that spans the boat, the boat is leveled athwartships at the bow. At this point (i.e., where the level is) a shore is placed from the shop floor to the bottom edge of the sheer strake (see Figure 7-1). The shore is screwed to the plank and a frame of the boat. A shore is similarly placed on the other side. The boat is then leveled and the shores nailed to the floor. Next, the boat is leveled and shored at the stern. Thus she is secured firmly in place and any possible twist is taken out of the hull.

Two cross spalls (see Figure 7-3) are then screwed into the sheer strake. These keep the boat's beam against the time when the molds are removed. The cross spalls are screwed down where the rowlock pads will be placed so that the screw holes will not be visible. The molds are then removed from the boat.

RIVETING

At this point the inside of the boat is bristling with copper nails (see Figure 7-2). These must be riveted, more nails put through the frames and riveted as well.

Holes are now drilled for all the remaining nails which go through the frames on the laps. These are no. 12 copper nails. All the nails are started and the frames rounded off on the inside. This is done with a concave scraper, whose shape is that of the rounded frame. Then, backing up with a weight on each frame, the nails are driven home to pull all together. Riveting on the frames is done in the usual way: burrs driven on with a burr set the nails cut off and headed over. The burrs are no. 13 driven over no. 12 nails; in other words, the burrs are one wire size smaller than the nails.

Figure 7-1. Dinghy shored up for finishing.

Figure 7-2. Inside of boat showing nails to be riveted.

Figure 7-3. Completely timbered out and riveted.

Riveting on the laps between the frames must now be done.
A smaller no. 14 copper nail is used here. No. 14 burrs
are dropped on all of the nails. This done, the excess
nail is cut off with a slight, quick, side-to-side rock-
ing motion of the cutters. This puts a flange on the
end of the nail which usually prevents the burr from fall-
ing off.* Thus one man prepared the whole boat for riveting and then called a helper and riveted up the boat in
several hours. If a burr does fall off, it is replaced
and held down with a thin wood chip while being riveted.

PUTTING IN THE BALANCE OF THE FLOORS AND FRAMES

Up to this point the boat has only every other floor and
frame pair in her and so the intervening floors are got
out and screwed to the keel.** The frames are then
steamed and as each frame comes out of the steam box, a
notch is cut out of an end for a limber, this being done
by eye. Then the frame is placed against the keel and a
small brass escutcheon pin nailed through the frame end
into the keel to hold the frame in place.*** The frame
is bent in and clamped (with a wooden clamp) to the sheer.
Its end is then firmly rapped with a hammer until it
bears on all of the planks.

Two to three nails are then bored for from the inside-
out and nails driven from the plank laps into the frame,

* In our case at Mystic, it did not and we did not mas-
ter this technique.

** It will be noted in all Herreshoff dinghies every
other floor is screwed from the keel into the floors and
the frames are riveted to these floors (these having been
bent on the molds), and the remaining floors are screwed
from the floor to the keel and their frames are screwed
into the floors (these having been put in after the boat
was turned right side up and the molds removed).

*** It was observed in our 1905 *Columbia* model lifeboat
dinghy that the brass escutcheon pins were still in place.
They were never removed. This points out one more thing
we were told by Charlie Sylvester -- anything which was
hidden, anything beneath the floor boards, for example,
was not finished. Frames were not rounded off, planks
not sanded, etc.

Figure 7-4. Putting in the inwale.

but not through the frame. When all of the frames are
thus put in and screwed to their respective floor timbers, their edges are rounded off with a scraper as far
as the floor boards would come. Anything beneath the
floor boards is not smoothly finished as it will not be
seen.

The rest of the holes for the copper nails are bored for
and the nails are then driven through the frames, the
burrs driven on, the nails cut off and riveted (see Figure 7-3).

The seat stringers (risers), seats, seat knees, breast
hook, quarter knees, and inwales are then put in. The
seat knees are steam-bent oak. They are oversize and
overbent so that a pattern could be put on and the knee
cut out. This proves to be an excellent and economical
way of obtaining seat knees.

In Herreshoff dinghies, the inwale is not tapered but is
of uniform width the length of the boat. It is notched
out for the quarter knees and breast hook as can be seen
in Figure 7-4. The inwale is riveted to the breast hook

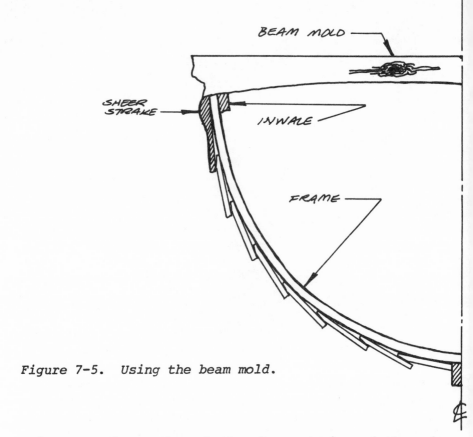

Figure 7-5. Using the beam mold.

and quarter knees through the sheer strake and through
each timber head.   No. 10 nails and no. 11 burrs are used
here.   It will be noted that fastening sizes were given
great thought, and they were always as light as was
deemed practical.

The frame tops are cut off and the whole planed to a
beam mold (see Figure 7-5).

When the boat is finished inside, she is turned over and
the plank laps are rounded off. This is done either with
a Stanley 101 or a specially made plane as shown in Figure 6-6 (page 31).

The rivets are then filed flush with the plank; as the
rivet heads are already sunk into the plank not much
had to be filed off. Mr. Sylvester had a special file
holder which put a convexity on the file face for doing
this job (see Figure 7-6).

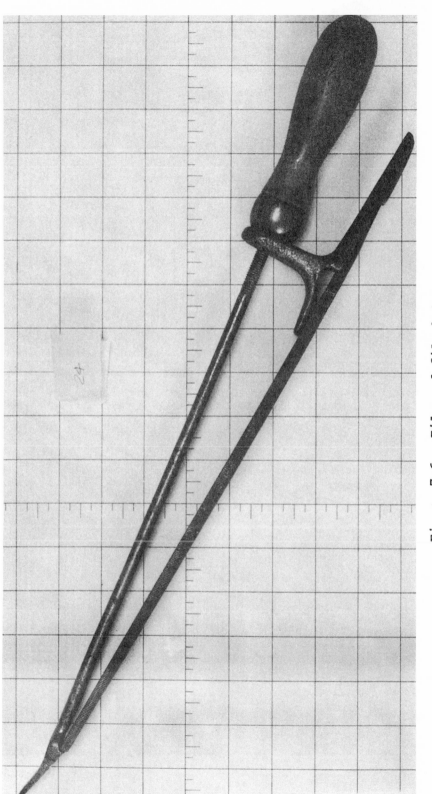

Figure 7-6. File and file holder.

Figure 8-1. New York 40 under construction.

44

B oats as large as the New York 50-footers, which were 72 feet overall, were built upside down with their frames bent over molds. Figure 8-1 shows a New York 40-footer under construction. Note there is a completed New York 40 hull in the background and a Fish class boat being built on the left. It can be seen that the New York 40 is double-planked and that a 2 x 2 is temporarily screwed to the hull so that the caulker can get up on the hull to caulk.

When finished, the New York 40 will be turned over and set on its keel. Figure 8-2 shows John Miller dubbing the deadwood (attached to its lead keel) of a 12 1/2-footer which will soon have a hull set on it.

In 1916, Rufus Murray, who had been in charge of the wood shop at Herreshoff's, went to Henry Nevins' at City Island. I have been told that it was "Ruf" Murray who really got Nevins set up. At any rate, Nevins

Figure 8-2. Dubbing a 12 1/2-footer deadwood.

Figure 8-4. Araminta, *frames bent over molds.*

built boats framed out over molds and upside down. So did Luders.

Charlie Sylvester called Fred Hodgdon the best planker he ever knew. Fred Hodgdon hailed from East Boothbay, Maine, where today his nephew, Sonny Hodgdon, prefers to build boats framed out over molds and where Norman Hodgdon built the boat shown in Figures 8-3 and 8-4.

Figure 8-3. *L. F. Herreshoff ketch* Araminta. *Floors on keel.*

Sailing Dingy

393 Rowboat

April 4 — Start 1931

Saturday · · · · · · · · · · · · · · hours

April 4		1
" 6		9
" 7		9
" 8		9
" 9		9
" 10		9
" 11	Saturday	5
" 13	Monday	9
" 14		9
" 15		9
" 16		9
" 17		9
" 18		4
" 20	Monday	8
" 21	Windy Repair	0
" 22		1½
23	Thursday	9
24	Friday	9
25	Sat.	Ventura Rowb
27	Monday	2½
	over	130

Charlie Sylvester's time and material

393

Stock

1   2" knee   stem
    9' western oak   keel
   14' 2" native oak   timbers
    4' native oak   floors timbers
    7' 1" teak   stern
    7' 2" Oak native .   boat knees
   79' 1" & 1¼" cedar Planking
   12' 1" teak . Sheer Strake
   20' 1¼" Cedar ?⊕ floor...
    4' 1" Western oak   centerboard box
    1   2" Hackmatack knee
                    quarter knee

   11' 1" teak Seats
    6' 1" teak Clamps
    4' 1" teak centerboard
    3' 1" teak Rudder
    8' spruce Spars

rep.

total for boat alone

account for a 10-foot 6-inch dinghy.

Photo Credits: Title Page - Ken Mahler; Contents Page -
Mary Anne Stets; Frontispiece I and II - Herreshoff
Collection at Mystic Seaport; p. 3 - L. F. Herreshoff
Collection at Mystic Seaport; p. 18 - Rob Pittaway; pp.
19, 22, 23 - Mary Anne Stets; pp. 29, 31, 32, 34, 35,
36 - Rob Pittaway; pp. 39, 41 - Mary Anne Stets; p. 43 -
Maynard Bray; p. 44, 45 - Herreshoff Collection at Mystic
Seaport; pp. 46, 47 - L. F. Herreshoff Collection at
Mystic Seaport

Drawings by Alison Pyott

Lines and Sail Plan by Rob Pittaway

Design by Behri P. Knauth